WIND IN THE WILLOWS™

THE MUSICAL BY MARK AND HELEN JOHNSON
SCRIPT BY SUE LANGWADE

A children's musical with twelve songs, in two acts.

Based on the classic story by Kenneth Grahame,
Retold in song and dance, drama and narrative.

For children aged 7-14 (KS2-3). Adaptable for all ages.

SONG LIST

(Please refer to the Music Book for piano arrangements and lyrics)

ACT ONE

OVERTURE		*Instrumental*
1.	Friends Together (Intro)	*Choir*
2.	Messing About In Boats	*Ratty, Mole and Choir*
3.	Bright Canary-Yellow Gypsy Caravan	*Ratty, Mole, Toad and Choir*
4.	It Takes All Sorts To Make A World	*Badger and Choir*
5.	Home Sweet Home	*Mole and Choir*
6.	King Of The Road	*Toad, Car Dealers and Choir*
7.	Twenty Years	*Chairman, Clerk, Toad and Choir*

ACT TWO

ENTR'ACTE		*Instrumental*
8.	Cheer Up Toad!	*Jailers Daughter, Toad and Choir*
9.	The Chase-Chase	*Toad, Train Driver(s), Police and Choir*
10.	We're The Stoats	*Stoats and Choir*
11.	He Can't Be Stopped!	*Toad and Choir*
12.	Life Of Luxury	*Weasels and Choir*
13.	Friends Together (Finale)	*All*

CAST OF CHARACTERS

Narrator
(This part, along with the other main parts, could be shared by 2 or more children)

Riverbank
Mole
Ratty
Toad
Badger
Otter
Rabbit
2 x Young Hedgehogs *(H/hog*)*
River People *(good diction)*
Ducks *(dancing)*
Assorted Woodland/Riverbank Creatures

Wild Wooders: (Rough and ready, sneaky types)
Chief Weasel (CW*)
Weasels 1-3 (W*)
Sarge Stoat
Harry
Bert
Stoats 1-7 *(SAS -Special Armed Stoats)*
Assorted additional Wild Wooders (Weasels/Stoats/Ferrets)
Trees *(non-speaking)*

Humans
Ethel
Jeeves
Sally *(jailer's daughter)*
2 x Train Drivers (TD*)
Rupert *(terribly upper class)*
Monica *(also terribly upper class)*
Policeman *('allo, 'allo, 'allo) (Pol*)*
Clerk *(solo singing part)*
2 x Delivery Men (DM*)
Salesman *(loud, somewhat pretentious) (SM*)*
2 x Prisoners *(tough characters) (Pris*)*
Chairman of the Board of Magistrates *(important solo singing)*
Train Passengers *(singing only)*
Police Train Passengers *(singing only)*
Jury/Court Crowd *(singing only)*
PR Girls *(singing only)*
Barge Woman *(non-speaking)*

** Indicates abbreviated name in script.*

ACT ONE

(Stage is set with a ladder, paint pot and brush, apron and duster and 'Home Sweet Home' sign either in front of the stage or at far side. To keep things simple, the backdrop could be a collage of the different locations, with perhaps a signpost indicating River/Wild Wood/Toad Hall etc. Minimal props can then be used as necessary to denote the individual locations. Various members of cast are gathered in groups; they mime chatting etc. Toad, Ratty, Mole and Badger are together, at the front.)

OVERTURE **CD Track 1**

SCENE 1: Riverside

Song 1 FRIENDS TOGETHER (INTRO) *(see Music Book, p66 for lyrics)* **CD Track 2**

(After song, begin to drift off in groups, except a few stoats and weasels, who hang around looking furtive. Toad, Ratty, Mole and Badger move to front of stage.)

Toad Well, well, we did have an adventure, didn't we chaps?

Ratty We certainly did, Toad old boy, we certainly did.

Mole I rather wish we could do it all again!

Badger My dear, young Mole, I think one adventure of that sort is enough for anybody's lifetime!

Ratty Ah, wise Badger! I'm sure you're right, as usual. But it was great fun!

Toad It was! And I can't think of three nicer chums to share such fun with! Dear Ratty, wise old Badger and sensible Moly. A chap couldn't ask for better friends!

Ratty I remember so clearly the day when it all began... Mole... you were I believe deep, deep down in the ground in your dear little home, cleaning it ready for spring. *(Mole goes off to ladder and duster)* And Badger, you were safely tucked away over in the worryingly Wild Wood...

All *(Tapping noses)* Where the stoats and weasels get up to no good!

Stoat 1 *(Moving forward)* Given half a chance! *(Snigger)*

Badger Away with you now! Shoo, shoo!

(Stoats exit.)

Ratty ...always ready to give a warm welcome!

Badger *(As he exits)* Why, thank you, Ratty dear boy.

Ratty *(Arm round Toad's shoulder – move to front centre stage)* And Toad... well, what can I say? Mr Toad, living a life of luxury in...

Toad ...Toad Hall, the finest house on the Riverbank!

Ratty Absolutely! Even though you say so yourself!

Toad At that time, dreaming of messing with boats not stoats! *(mimes rowing off)* Handy having a friend like you Ratty living by the river. *(Exit)*

Ratty By it and with it and on it and in it! It's my brother and sister, family and friend! Food and drink... oh and *(Sniffing himself)* washing of course! It's my world and I wouldn't want any other! *(Exit)*

(Enter Narrator. He should have script concealed within a large copy of 'Wind in the Willows'. Mole begins cleaning.)

Narr I say, shall I help you along as our tale gets underway? I can fill in some gaps so it's not too long a play! Okay. The adventure began with our four friends in their beloved homes, safe and sound. Madly polishing and dusting, Mole worked underground. But in the air above and in the earth below, spring was moving –

(Woodland Creatures enter, quietly giggling and chasing.)

Mole *(Coughing with dust)* Bother! O blow!

Narr So when the wind in the willows whispered his name, Mole couldn't resist ...

Mole Hang spring-cleaning! *(Throws down duster etc)*

Narr ... and up he came – with a scrabble and a scrooge and an...

Mole Up we go! *(Mole mimes scrambling upwards, rolls onto stage)*

Narr ... till he found himself rolling in a warm, great meadow.

(Woodland Creatures do an appropriate movement eg: lambs gambol; frogs leap; rabbits hop; rats roll, whilst calling out the relevant word. Mole joins in with them, thoroughly enjoying himself, until he suddenly freezes, transfixed by something. All then freeze, staring in the direction of the river, which will vary according to the lay out of the stage. River People enter and move across a defined area, which will be the 'river space' for the next scene.)

Narr Mole had thought his happiness complete until he saw... a full-fed river. Never before had he seen a river. Such an awesome sight! Now he gazed, entranced, at this sleek, powerful, twisting animal, which sparkled in the morning light.

(Enter River People, dressed in silvers and blues, perhaps with 'cloaks' of water-like fabric. They move slowly, rhythmically across stage, depending on available area. The following dialogue should be 'shared out', as it would be difficult to speak in unison.)

River Sleek and twisting; chasing, chuckling; gurgling, glints and gleams;
A-shake and a-shiver, meanders the river through your hopes and dreams.
Chatter and bubble; through laughter and trouble; faithful, foaming friend.
Sparkle and swirl to who knows where, as the seasons come and the seasons go
And you watch my everlasting flow, round bend after chuckling bend.
The willows bow to my majesty, dipping tips to sip of my foam.
And they whisper tales of the rats and voles who call this river home.

(As River exits, Ratty enters, followed by Ducks who move into 'river space', downstage of Ratty and Mole, miming swimming in various formations. Woodland Creatures could exit or remain in background if wanted for next song. Mole still stands entranced.)

Ratty *(Trying to break him out of trance)* Hello Mole!

Mole *(Suddenly back to earth)* Hello Rat.

Ratty I say, how would you like to come over and join me for a picnic?

Mole *(Gesturing to the 'water')* Well, that's easy for you to say!

Ratty Aha! *(He fetches a boat and rows it across to Mole)* Now then step lively!

Mole Oh I say! O my! What a wonderful day! I've never been in a boat before. Is it nice?

Ratty What? Never been in a boat!! Is it nice?! Why, it's the only thing! Believe me my young friend: there is nothing, absolutely nothing, half so much worth doing as messing about in boats; simply messing about in boats!

Song 2 MESSING ABOUT IN BOATS *(see Music Book, p67 for lyrics)* **CD Track 3**
(This is an opportunity for a choreographed Duck Dance in the background!)

Ratty Moly, why don't you come and stay with me for a while? It's plain and rough, but it's snug and comfortable. We could have such fun. I could teach you to row and to swim!

Mole Oh Ratty, I'd love to! How kind you are!

(Row to side of stage, put boat away and bring on folding chairs and picnic. Ratty and Mole relax and enjoy the picnic. Ducks exit.)

Narr A deal was struck, a friendship forged. *(Ratty and Mole shake hands)* A jolly time was had by all, as the ripening summer unfolded for the mole.

Ratty Listen to my latest song, Moly old boy! It's about the ducks:

All along the backwater,
Through the rushes tall,
Ducks are a-dabbling,
Up tails all!

Mole *(Distracted)* Yes, yes, wonderful,. Ratty, I wonder if I might ask you a favour?

Ratty Of course, dear fellow.

Mole You've told me so much about Toad. I would really like to meet him.

Ratty No problem, Moly. We shall go right away. I can sing you the rest of my song on the way.

(Ratty and Mole exit. Enter 2 Stoats, Harry and Bert.)

Bert *(With Cockney accent)* I say, I say, I say 'arry – does that look like a picnic to you?

Harry It does, Bert.

Bert 'Ere, 'arry. What do you get if you cross two stoats with a picnic?

Harry I don't know, Bert, what do you get if you cross two stoats with a picnic? – Crumbs maybe?

Bert A pic-nicked! *(They run off sniggering, taking the picnic stuff)*

SCENE CHANGE MUSIC **CD2 Track 17**

SCENE 2: Toad Hall Exterior
(Caravan is set – could be made up of children, or Ethel and Jeeves bring on 2-D caravan front.)

Ethel I don't know! What are we to do with Mr Toad? Once it was sailing, then he tired of that and took to punting.

Jeeves And a nice mess he made of that!

Ethel Last year it was house-boating. He was going to spend the rest of his life in a houseboat!

Jeeves Then he got a 'sinking feeling' about that! *(He nudges Ethel who doesn't respond)* Anyhow, it's always the same with Mr Toad – whatever he takes up, he soon gets tired of it and starts on something new. Now this – a caravan! Whatever next? Pass me that bacon, would you?

(During following dialogue, E & J keep putting things into caravan (into a box for easy removal later!) A crate of drinks is left at the side of the caravan. Mole and Ratty enter through audience.)

Mole Are you sure Mr Toad won't mind our dropping in like this?

Ratty It's never the wrong time to call on Toad. Early or late he's always the same fellow – always good tempered.

Mole He must be a very nice animal.

Ratty He is indeed the best of animals.

(Toad enters singing a snatch from 'Bright Canary-Yellow Gypsy Caravan'.)

Toad Why Ratty, welcome, welcome! And your good friend Mole – how splendid to see you! I was about to send for you. Come along, come along both of you. I've got something so exciting to show you!

(Move onto stage. Jeeves and Ethel exit.)

Toad Ta da! There you are! There's real life for you embodied in that little cart! The Open Road! The Dusty Highway! Here today, somewhere else tomorrow! Travel, change, <u>excitement</u>! Everything's in it – all ready for us to make a start this afternoon!

Ratty <u>Us</u>? This after<u>noon</u>? I don't think so, Toad! <u>I'm</u> not going anywhere!

Toad Ratty, surely you don't want to stick to your dull, smelly old river all your life! I want to show you the world. I'm going to make an animal of you, my boy!

Ratty Actually Toad, I <u>do</u> want to stick to my dull, smelly old river – and Mole will stick with <u>me</u>, won't you Mole?

Mole Of course, I'll always stick with you, Ratty. All the same, it does look rather fun.

Toad We needn't decide anything in a hurry! I don't really care either way. I just thought you might enjoy it that's all. 'Live for others' – that's my motto in life! *(Winking very obviously at Mole)* Why don't we go and have a spot of lunch and we can talk it over?

(As they exit, Toad collects drinks crate.)

SCENE CHANGE MUSIC **CD2 Track 17**

SCENE 3: Country Road
(Bushes are brought on, concealing various Woodland Creatures. Enter Toad, Mole and Ratty. Enter Woodland Creature 1 playing hide and seek. S/he stops when s/he sees cart.)

WC1 Ready or not, here I come... Oh my, oh my, oh my!

WC2 *(Popping up from behind bush)* That <u>is</u> a beautiful cart, Mr Toad!

WC3 It's the 'beautifullest' cart I've ever seen! Let's go and tell the others! *(They run off)*

Toad *(To Ratty and Mole)* There now, aren't you glad you came? A life on the open road, there's nothing like it! And there's certainly nothing like our wonderful yellow caravan!

Song 3 BRIGHT CANARY-YELLOW GYPSY CARAVAN *(see Music Book, p68 for lyrics)* **CD Track 4**
(Toad, Ratty and Mole sit travelling upon the caravan whilst singing this song.)

(Woodland Creatures gather, admiring caravan. During the following narration a car is driven on. 'SFX Car and caravan crash' is heard (as indicated) as the narration continues. The car moves swiftly across stage, knocking the caravan over en route.)

Narr The sun shone golden, the birds sweetly sung! Adventure beckoned; they had hardly begun...

Toad *(Breathing deeply)* Ah! This is the life!

Narr ...when their ears pricked up to a faint warning hum, like the drone of a distant bee.

SFX **Car and caravan crash** *(continue following dialogue and action over SFX)* **CD2 Track 18**

Ratty Whatever is that noise?

Narr Then all of a sudden, a <u>car</u> was upon 'em, with a blast of wind and a whirl of sound, that knocked their feet right off the ground, the dust too thick for them to see! 'Poop-poop! Poop-poop!' rang in their ears, then as suddenly as it had come, the car disappeared!

Ratty *(Shaking his fist)* You villains! You scoundrels! You road hogs!

(Mole and Ratty try to right the cart. Toad sits in the middle of the stage in a dreamlike state.)

Toad *(As though in a trance)* Poop-poop! Poop-poop!

Ratty Toad, come and give us a hand!

Toad Poop-poop! Glorious stirring sight! The poetry of motion. The real way to travel. Here today, in next week tomorrow! Oh my, oh my!

Ratty Oh dear, oh dear!

Mole Whatever's the matter with him?

Ratty Toad is now possessed. He has a new craze. There's nothing to be done. He'll be like that for days now. Let's get him out of here.

Toad Poop-poop! Poop-poop!

(They drag him off. If children have 'made up' car, they roll off. Ethel and Jeeves arrive to pick up the pieces! If extra hands are needed, they can be children in T-shirts marked 'ACME RECOVERY'. Scene can be changed during the following dialogue.)

Ethel Well I never! Didn't we just know this would end in tears?

Jeeves Not that Mr Toad is crying! He's as happy as a lark!

Ethel Why's that then?

Jeeves Can't you guess? He's just been to Parper and Parpers and ordered a great big, expensive motor-car!

Ethel Heaven help us all! *(Both exit.)*

SCENE 4: Wild Wood
(With chair to indicate Ratty's home – use Scene Change Music if more time is required to change scenes.)

(Ratty enters, bringing on chair. He dozes in it at front of stage. There needs to be a coat and hat each for Mole and Ratty. During following narration, Mole paces up and down, writes a note, dons hat and coat and tiptoes out.)

Narr When winter came, Ratty was a very sleepy rat. Mole, finding himself with much time to spare, wrote a note then donned his coat and hat. Leaving Ratty snoozing by a bright and blazing fire, and against all good advice, he set off for The Wild Wood.

S & W *(Popping heads either side of stage)* Where us stoats and weasels get up to no good! *(Sniggering)*

Narr Mole's longing to meet Badger overcame all sense of caution and off he strode, under a hard and steely sky, along a barren, wintry country road. *(Exit)*

(Enter group of Wild Wooders: the following is chanted.)

WWs We are the Wild Wooders and we prowl The Wild Wood
We slink in shade and shadows 'cos we're all up to no good!
We pick on smaller creatures 'cos it's such a jolly jape,
We love it when they shiver and they quiver and they quake.

(Hear Mole approaching and hide among trees.)

SFX **The Wild Wood** *(continues playing until SFX OFF is indicated)* **CD2 Track 19**

(Trees begin to gather, building up into a thick wood. Occasionally, WWs scurry across the stage; popping out very quickly to deliver lines and then hide again. Whispers/pattering etc. Mole enters looking very nervous.)

Mole Oh, I wish I knew where I was!

WWs *(Appearing then disappearing very quickly)* Ooooooo!

(Mole jumps.)

Narr Deeper and deeper went Mole into the darkness, where the trees crouched nearer and nearer, and holes made ugly mouths!

WWs *(Behind Mole's back)* Boo!

Narr Then – a face! But he turned and it was gone.

WWs Yoo hoo!

Narr Then, hundreds of them – one by one by one – all fixing on him glances of malice and hatred, all hard-eyed and evil and sharp!

Rabbit *(Running across and nearly bumping into Mole)* Get out of this you fool! Get out! *(Exit)*

Narr Now, whistling and pattering. In front or behind? He couldn't tell. At last he took refuge in the dark, deep hollow of an old beech tree. How he wanted to yell! But his mouth was dry; his cry was silenced; silenced by the very terror of The Wild Wood!

(Wild Wooders laugh. Mole huddles at the foot of one of the trees, shaking and whimpering. SFX OFF.)

Ratty *(Stretching and yawning)* What a wonderful dream! Messing about on my boat! Time for a bite of supper. What do you say, Mole old chap? Moly! Moly! *(Finding note)* Why, what's this? My poor dear Mole! *(Puts on own coat etc and picks up cudgel, then exits and re-appears other side or through audience)*

SFX **The Wild Wood** *(continue until SFX OFF)* **CD2 Track 19**

Ratty Moly, Moly Moly! Where are you? It's me – it's old Rat!

(There is some scurrying across stage.)

Ratty *(Holding weapon up)* Don't even think about it! Moly! Moly!

Mole Over here! Over here! My dear Ratty! I've been so frightened I can't tell you!

Ratty Oh I quite understand. But I'm here now! Come on – let's make a start for home.

Mole *(Tries to stand up but almost faints)* Dear Ratty, please forgive me but I'm so very tired. You must let me rest for a while.

Ratty All right, Moly, you rest away. It's nearly pitch dark now – there ought to be a bit of a moon later. Let's settle down here for now.

(Both lie down. During narration, trees could be draped in strips of white fabric/crepe paper.)

SCENE 4a: Wild Wood covered in snow

Narr But the light that later gleamed and glistened on the ground was not just from the moon, but from it's light reflecting on snow. They found, when they awoke, a scene transformed by a blanket of white. There seemed to be no end to this wood, no beginning and, worst of all, no way out!

Mole Oh dear, Ratty. It all looks the same!

Ratty Let's try this way.

Mole I'm sure we've been that way before.

Ratty How about this way then?

Mole Oh, it's impossible! *(Mole trips)* Ow!

Ratty Poor Moly, you're not having much luck today. What did you trip on? Oh I say, look here! This is a door knocker! Yes! *(Dances a jig)*

Mole You find a piece of old junk and you dance a jig around it! Really Rat!

Ratty And here's a doormat! A doormat! Hurray!

Mole I think that's enough of this folly! What good is a doormat? Can we eat a doormat? Can we ride home on a doormat?

Ratty Look, you dull-witted animal! *(Uncovering a sign)*

Mole MR BADGER! Why Ratty, you're a wonder! A real wonder, that's what you are!

(They knock on door and freeze until SFX OFF and music starts.)

SCENE CHANGE MUSIC **CD2 Track 17**

SCENE 5: Badger's House
(Trees exit, Ratty's chair removed as narration continues. Badger's table/fire set. Enter Otter and two nervous looking hedgehogs, who are carrying food which Otter keeps picking at.)

Otter There now, young 'uns, nothing to be nervous about. I know Badger can seem a gruff sort of chap, but underneath it all, he's as generous and kind a fellow as you could ever hope to meet. And his larder's always so well stocked! *(Nibbling food)*

Narr In the chilling Wild Wood, if anyone could be relied upon to provide a warm fire, a warm meal and a warm welcome, Mr Badger could!

H/hog 1 Mr Badger founded us when we was lost coming home from school.

Otter Found us when we were lost.

H/hog 2 Oh, we didn't know you was lost as well, Mr Otter!

Otter Oh, never mind, just pass me a large chunk of cheese, would you?

(Enter Badger, Ratty and Mole.)

Badger Come and get yourselves warm. Poor Mole, you look positively pale and that's quite something for a mole!

Ratty I just cannot believe the nerve of those Wild Wooders, trying to scare our poor friend here half to death! I don't know how you can live here among them, Badger, really I don't! Villains the lot of 'em!

Badger Now, now Ratty! They're not all bad, you know. They're just like any other animal – some good, some bad. Actually, I rather like the variety – wouldn't do if we were all the same now, would it!

Song 4 IT TAKES ALL SORTS TO MAKE A WORLD *(see Music Book, p69 for lyrics)* **CD Track 5**

(During instrumental verse:)

Mole Oh Mr Badger, it's so good to be back underground! This is a wonderful home you have here!

Badger Why, thank you Mole. I'm glad you like it. Let me show you round – there are tunnels enough to satisfy anybody! *(Take Mole round stage, pointing)*

Ratty You know, Otter, glad as I am to see Badger, I just couldn't be doing with not having a window or two for very long!

Otter Me neither, Ratty – and a constant food supply swimming by, of course!

Ratty Ah, the good old Riverbank!

Mole Ah, deep underground!

Tog There's no place like it!

(After song they move to table and sit down.)

Badger Come and eat some supper. Good gracious, I'd better re-stock the table – these young rascals have nearly eaten me out of house and sett! *(Otter looks away innocently stuffing something into his mouth)* Now then, tell us the news from your part of the world. How's old Toad going on?

Mole It's terribly scary. He had another smash up last week – a bad one! He will insist on driving but he's really not safe!!

Otter How many has he had?

Ratty Cars or smashes? Actually with Toad it's the same thing! This is the seventh. He'll either be killed or bankrupt before too long. Don't you think we should do something about it, Badger?

Badger Once the weather has turned and the nights are shorter, we – that's you, me and our friend Mole here – will take Toad in hand. We'll stand no nonsense whatsoever. We'll <u>make</u> him be a sensible Toad! After all, what are friends for?

(All exit, taking props if poss. Remove table etc.)

Narr The following day, refreshed by friendship and food, Ratty and Mole set off through a series of secret tunnels, leading them to the edge of the wood.

(Enter Ratty and Mole in outdoor clothes.)

Mole You know, Ratty – seeing Badger's lovely underground home reminded me of my own little place. It's very rough, but it's mine and I do miss it. Sometimes I think I can almost smell it. *(Sniffs)* In fact, I think I can now! Yes! I'm sure I can. Come on Ratty! This way!

(Whilst Ratty and Mole are sniffing out Mole's house, the stage is reset as in Scene 1.)

SCENE 6: Mole End

Ratty What can you smell, Moly – old socks, some cheese you left rotting? *(Sniffing towards audience)* Definitely something cheesy over here!

Mole Home, that's what I can smell Ratty! Home. And here it is, just as I left it. Mole End! Home sweet home!

Song 5 HOME SWEET HOME *(see Music Book, p70 for lyrics)* **CD Track 6**

Mole I am looking forward to getting back to the Riverbank, Ratty, but I will miss this little place.

Ratty Nevermind, Moly, it'll always be here for you whenever you need it. That's the wonderful thing about home: it's not just a place you go back to – it's somewhere you carry round in your heart.

(Exit. Mole's house is taken off.)

Narr Seasons have gone, seasons have come. Now the bleak midwinter's given way to the high summer sun. I say, doesn't time fly when you're having fun?

SCENE 7: Riverside
(Enter Badger, followed by Ratty and Mole. Badger moves centre stage and makes a forceful announcement.)

Badger The Hour has come!

Ratty What hour?

Badger Why, Toad's hour! The Hour of Toad! I said I'd take him in hand as soon as the winter was fully over and I'm going to take him in hand today!

Mole Toad's hour, of <u>course</u>! Hooray! I remember now. <u>We'll</u> make him a sensible toad!

Badger This very morning a new and very powerful motor-car is being delivered to Toad Hall on sale or return. We must make haste and rescue Toad from himself before it's too late!

Ratty Right you are! We'll rescue the poor unhappy animal. We'll change him. He'll be the most changed toad ever!

SCENE 8: Toad Hall Exterior
(Enter 2 Delivery Men with 2-D car, followed a moment later by a Salesman with a bottle of champagne and a couple of PR Girls with clipboards on which are forms for Toad to sign.)

DM1 This must be the place. Look at all the skid marks and all the bits of car over there! He's known as 'Towed Away' of Toad Hall now. Get it? Not that there's usually much left to tow!

DM2 'E's a real menace! It's a good job for 'im Helf and Safety 'aven't been invented yet!

SM Where is he then? Where's our best customer! At Parper and Parper, we like to reward our most loyal clients! *(Enter Toad.)* Ah, Mr Toad! You've chosen a good 'un this time, you have. Top of the range this sir, cream de la cream *(pronounced 'cream', not 'crème')* of motor-cars. Every conceivable gadget going! This is very 20th Century!

DM1 He'd be better off with a tank.

DM2 I don't think so. There'd be nothing left standing between here and ___________ *(Local place)*!

SM Let me just show you what we have here. This, Mr Toad, is nothing less than the future! Why not try it for size?

Song 6 KING OF THE ROAD *(see Music Book, p71 for lyrics)* **CD Track 7** or **CD2 Track 16**
(After song, Badger, Ratty and Mole enter.)

Badger *(Pushing SM & DM off)* I'm sorry, Mr Toad won't be needing any more vehicles thank you! At least that one can go back in one piece.

Toad No! No! What are you doing? Come back. I <u>need</u> my car!

(They hold him back.)

Badger You knew it must come to this sooner or later, Toad. We have warned you, but you've gone on wasting the money your father left you. You're getting us animals a bad name with the way you drive and crash and row with the police! We animals never allow our friends to make fools of themselves for too long and your time is up! You and I are going to have a little chat!

(Badger and Toad exit. Mole and Ratty pace up and down.)

Mole Do you really think he'll see sense, Ratty?

Ratty If he'll listen to anyone, it's Badger. He was a great friend of Toad's father, you know. Claws crossed old fellow!

(Badger and Toad re-enter.)

Badger Here we are. One Toad who will be staying well away from motor-cars!

Ratty Oh, well done Badger! And good for you Toad! No more motor-cars, eh?

Toad I <u>will</u> have a motor-car! I <u>will</u>! Poop-poop! Poop-poop!

Badger But Toad, you promised!

Toad Oh yes, in <u>there</u>! I'd have said anything in <u>there!</u> But out here... with the delicious smell of car fumes still in the air! No! I want my car! You can't stop me! I want my car, I want my car!

(He is taken off by the scruff of the neck by B, R & M. Thereafter periodical hysterical wailing and crying is heard off stage. Enter Ethel and Jeeves, in outdoor clothes, ready to go to town.)

Ethel It's hard to listen to all that screaming and wailing! It's been days now! I don't know how his friends can stand it! I don't wonder Mr Badger and Mr Mole have had to go off for the day for a break! Poor Mr Rat! If only Mr Toad would promise not to go near a motor-car again!

Jeeves You know what he's like! He won't give in easily. He's far too used to getting his own way. Anyway, we'd better hurry if we're going to catch that bus into town and get more supplies. *(More wailing)* Better add a few more boxes of tissues to the list!

(During the following narration, a knotted sheet appears from side of stage. Toad 'climbs' down it on hands and knees.)

Narr Toad's friends had determined to keep Toad safely under lock and key until the spell which motor-cars had cast over him was broken. We'll see!

Toad I'm not a prisoner, I'm a clever toad! *(Runs off)*

Narr Uh oh! Devious Toad is off down the road, whistling a merry tune. Alas, poor Toad! He's not free, for he's still bound to the dreaded motor-car, which could prove his downfall all too soon!

(2-D car enters across stage driven by Rupert and Monica. From side of stage pub notice appears 'The Red Lion'. Car is 'parked' and R&M enter pub.)

Rupert G & T for you, darling?

Monica Just a little one though – I don't want to get squiffy!

(Toad appears, sees car, becomes ecstatic, looks around furtively, gets in and steals car. Drives off shouting 'Poop-poop!' If there is room, he could drive around the audience before crashing.)

Narr Once at the wheel, Toad knew only that he was Toad once more. Toad at his best and highest. Toad the Terror, lord of the lone trail!

Rupert *(Running out of pub)* I say, he's stolen my car! Stop thief!

SFX **Car crash** **CD2 Track 20**
(Rupert reacts. Enter policeman dragging a dishevelled Toad.)

Pol 'Allo, 'allo, 'allo! What 'ave we 'ere?

Toad Unhand me you ruffian! Don't you know who I am, you nincompoop!

Pol I don't care who you are. But I know where you're going – jail!

SCENE CHANGE MUSIC **CD2 Track 17**

SCENE 9: Court
(Set Court scene. Jury members come bustling in, chattering amongst themselves. Clerk and other magistrates enter. Toad is brought on handcuffed.)

Clerk *(Tapping his gavel on bench)* Order! Order! Silence! Please be upstanding for his honour the Chairman of the Bench of Magistrates! *(Enter Chairman)*

Song 7 TWENTY YEARS *(see Music Book, p72 for lyrics)* **CD Track 8**

INTERVAL

ACT TWO

ENTR'ACTE **CD Track 9**

SCENE 1: Jail

(Toad is in jail. There are two other prisoners in an adjoining cell. To help with sightlines, they could be seated on wooden benches rather than the floor.)

Toad This is the end of everything! At least it is the end of the career of Toad which is the same thing. The popular and handsome Toad, the rich and hospitable Toad, the Toad so free and careless and debonair! How can I hope to ever be set at large again!

Pris 1 Would you Adam and Eve it? He's orf again! Why don't you give your poor teeth a rest?

Pris 2 Yeah – and our ears!

Pris 1 Didn't feel like we was doin' 'ard time till you got 'ere!

Toad I am a toad accustomed to giving inspirational speeches! Oh! Never again will I entertain all my friends with my wit and wisdom!

Sally There, there Mr Toad, don't go on so. It's not the end of the world! Look what I've brought for you!

Song 8 CHEER UP TOAD! *(see Music Book, p74 for lyrics)* **CD Track 10**

(During instrumental verse:)

Pris 1 'Ere Sally – you should have made 'im Toad in the 'ole!

Pris 2 No! Babble and squeak!

Sally Hush you two, can't you see he's upset?

Pris 1 Oh there, there Mr Toad! Have a nice cuppa char!

Pris 2 *(Holding up little finger)* Don't forget your 'pinkie'.

Sally Come on, Mr Toad, give us a smile – you know you want to! Haven't you got a nice smile for Sally? Oh, what am I gonna do with you?!

Sally I know what might really cheer you up. I think I may know how you could escape. My aunt is the washerwoman here at the prison. If you could see your way clear to giving her a few bob, I'm sure she'd let you borrow her dress and bonnet and so on, and then you could leave the prison suitably disguised!

Toad Surely you wouldn't have Toad of Toad Hall go about the country dressed as a washerwoman?!

Sally Then you can stop here as a toad! I suppose you want to go off in a horse-driven coach!

Toad *(Repentant)* You are a good, kind, clever girl and I am a proud and stupid toad. Introduce me to your worthy aunt and I have no doubt we will be able to come to some satisfactory arrangement.

(During the following narration, Sally dresses Toad as washerwoman.)

Narr And so the great escape was planned, a certain sum of money changing hands. A dress and shawl and bonnet were duly bestowed. Well, there's a washerwoman, wherever is Mr Toad?

(Sally and other prisoners exit, looking happy and taking any removable set/staging. Toad mimes the following action, nodding and reacting to imaginary people as he goes.)

Narr A shaking, quaking Toad set forth, but his disguise was a passport for every barred door! Unsure at one point which way to go, he was helped by a warder, anxious to get home for his tea. A few more bold steps and... fresh air. He was free!

SFX **Jail door** **CD2 Track 21**

(Train station sign goes up. Crowd begins to gather.)

Toad Right, I need to get away from here as fast as I can. Where's my wallet? Oh no! I left it with my jacket back in the cell.

(Enter Train Drivers with 2-D train front.)

TD 2 All aboard!

SFX **Train whistle** **CD2 Track 22**

(People gather in a 'train carriage' formation behind TD and when train starts off they do 'chugging' motion with their arms. They could also make the relevant sound.)

Toad *(Wailing)* Oh dear, oh dear!

TD 1 Why, whatever's the matter, mother?

Toad I'm a poor washerwoman and I've lost all my money and if I don't get home to my children tonight, there's no knowing what they'll get up to. They'll be playing with matches and upsetting lamps and they'll be so hungry. Oh dear, oh dear!

TD 1 There, there, old woman. I'll tell you what I'll do. You're a washerwoman, right? Then you take some of my shirts to wash and send them back to me all nice and clean, like, and I'll let you ride on my train. How about that?

Toad You are so kind, sir!

TD 2 All set. Off we go! *(Blows whistle)*

(Train chugs off. Station sign is taken down. After a few moments a police train comes up behind. During the following song, there is opportunity for audience participation, with certain lyrics being displayed and 'policeman plants' being placed in or around the audience – for more details, please see Song Performance Tips, page 6.)

Song 9 THE CHASE-CHASE *(see Music Book, p75 for lyrics)* **CD Track 11**
(We've included a Words on Screen™ version of this song on the enhanced CD element of CD 2 – a great tool if you want to get the audience involved!)

Toad Ha ha! Clever Toad! Once again – fooled 'em all! Ha ha! *(Runs off)*

SCENE 2: Country Road
(Enter Ratty, Mole and Badger, who is bandaged up. He and Mole look dishevelled and shaken.)

Ratty How are you feeling now, Badger? Those blasted Wild Wooders. I knew it! Cowards the lot of 'em – just like all bullies! If I could just get hold of 'em now...

Badger I'm not feeling so bad Ratty. My pride hurts more than anything else. We tried our best! We were just outnumbered!

Mole We were lucky to get out alive! Fancy those Wild Wooders throwing us out of Toad Hall and taking it over. I didn't think even they'd stoop to that!

Badger I just can't bear the thought of all those ruffians messing up Toad Hall. Toad's worthy father will be turning in his grave! Such a stately place!

Ratty I don't know about stately, but I'm pretty sure it'll be in a state by now! They'll have taken full advantage of Toad's well stocked larder and cellar. It's just a small blessing that Toad doesn't know anything about it!

Mole Yes! Poor Mr Toad. I wonder how he's getting on? *(Exit)*

Narr Poor Mr Toad is still journeying home. This poor, ingenious Toad hitched a lift on a barge! But when she rumbled his disguise, with blazing eyes, the barge woman – a rather large woman – threw him overboard! Oh Lord! Is he full of remorse? No! He's stolen her horse!

SFX **Neddy, the horse** **CD2 Track 23**
(Toad runs across/in front of stage on a hobby horse.)

Toad *(Shouting towards side of stage)* Ha! That'll teach you, you rotten old barge woman. Fancy throwing Toad of Toad Hall off your old barge! See how far you get now without old Neddy here! He should fetch a bob or two and buy me a nice bite to eat! Ha! Toad, my boy, you are a genius! Gee up Neddy! *(Exit)*

SCENE 3: Toad Hall Exterior
(Enter SAS – Special Armed Stoats – marching. Sarge leads them in.)

Sarge Hup, two, three... *(counts on his fingers – can't work out what comes next so)*... hup, two, three and hup, two, three and hup, two, three and halt! About turn. *(All face front except one)* You silly little stoat! I said about turn! *(All others turn other way and offender now faces front. Leader moves to front)* All just turn and look at me! What am I going to do with you lot?!

Stoat 1 Manoeuvres, Sarge. That's what you said before. You said we'd come out here and...

Sarge *(Tempted to hit him but keeps his temper)* That's right – manoeuvres! Let's see how much you've remembered! *(The stoats get into relevant poses and do various kung fu type moves, with accompanying sounds, as Sarge calls out the following:)* Sneaky Stoat; Scary Stoat; Slithering Stoat, Chop Suey Stoat!

That's better! Anyone trying to get into the Chief Weasel's party tonight had better look out! They won't get past us! We're the stoats! Who are we?

All We're the stoats! *(If possible, Stoat 1 says this line marginally later than the other stoats)*

Sarge *(Louder)* Who are we?

All *(Louder)* We're the Stoats! *(Stoat 1 later, as before)*

Song 10 WE'RE THE STOATS *(see Music Book, p77 for lyrics)* **CD Track 12**
(During song they do tango/staccato moves with their weapons, with Stoat 1 occasionally going the wrong way.)

Sarge *Company, about turn! (Except Stoat 1. Sarge goes and physically turns him round) There's always one! And hup, two, three and hup, two, three. (All exit)*

SCENE 4: Toad Hall Interior

(As the Stoats exit a banner is hung reading 'Happy Birthday Chief!' Chief Weasel and entourage enter.)

CW Happy birthday to me, happy birthday to me, happy birthday Chief Weasel, happy birthday to me! Oh yes – this was definitely one of my better plans, invading Toad Hall. Nice one Cyril!

W1 Yeah nice one Cyril!

CW *(Twisting W1's ear)* Chief to you sonny! Show some respect – R E S T P E... R E P K E... Respect do you hear?

W1 Sir, yes sir! Er... Chief, yes Chief!

CW How're the arrangements coming along for my surprise party?

W3 Everything's almost ready Chief.

CW Very good. I'm going to be very touched I'm sure. Make sure my best suit is clean and pressed. I do like to impress the ladies, you know.

W3 There won't be any ladies there Chief, only your girlfriend and her ferret friends... *(W2 thumps him)*

W2 *(Quickly)* You should have your portrait done, Chief – like what all them toads have done – you know, them ones in the old-fashioned gear in that big 'all: Richard the Toad, William Webberforce, Andrew Toad-Webber...

CW The former residents of this fine place, I believe. They're history now – just like our friend Mr Toad – gawd bless him, wherever he may be! *(Exit, laughing)*

Narr Oh, he's back on the road – the unstoppable Toad!

SCENE 5: Country Road
(The birthday banner should be removed. Toad enters driving car with two passengers, Rupert and Monica.)

Toad Thank you so much for giving an old washerwoman a lift and letting her drive your lovely car. Oooh, I wonder what this pedal does?

Rupert You want to go easy on that pedal Madam!

Monica Help, help! Oh my hat!

(Toad presses down hard, they whizz off stage.)

SFX **Car crash** **CD2 Track 20**
(A wheel rolls onto the stage.)

Rupert *(Off stage)* Which way did she go? Dash it, I think we've lost her!

Toad *(Running on, out of breath)* Oh my! I think I've lost them at last! Fancy getting that worked up about a little smash! They should have had more sense than to let an old washerwoman like me drive their car! *(Laughs heartily)* Once again, you've given them the slip old boy! There's just no stopping you!

Song 11 HE CAN'T BE STOPPED! *(see Music Book, p78 for lyrics)* **CD Track 13**
(Woodland Creatures could enter to join in. At end of song all exit.)

SCENE CHANGE MUSIC **CD2 Track 17**

SCENE 6: Ratty's House
(Table set with tea. Ratty, Mole and Badger seated.)

Ratty Here you are, Badger, a nice cup of tea!

Badger Thank you, Ratty, that's just what...

Toad *(Bursting in)* Oh! You're all here, how marvellous!

All Toad!

Toad Yes, Toad! The one and only, the brilliant, ingenious, train hopping, car stopping Toad! Just wait till I tell you what I've been up to. My friends, you are in the presence of a genius! This deserves a celebration! If you can lend me some clothes I'll get back to Toad Hall and arrange a banquet fit for such an incredible Toad and you shall all come and hear...

Ratty Toad! That's quite enough! We have something important to tell you. I'm afraid you can't go back to Toad Hall. A large band of stoats and weasels has taken it over!

Toad Oh no! How could you let that happen? After all I've been through! Now this!

Mole We did everything we could! And if you weren't so pleased with yourself, you might have noticed poor Badger and the knocks he got trying to stop them!

Toad *(Wailing)* Oh, I am a selfish, thoughtless Toad! Badger, I'm so sorry! But what am I going to do? Oh, this is the end of everything!

Badger There might be something we can do. We need to keep our heads and make a plan. They have guards everywhere, but I think I might have an idea... Toad, go and get some proper clothes on then we'll work something out. *(Toad exits)* Now, if I remember rightly, Toad's father showed me a secret way into Toad Hall. He didn't want Toad to know unless it was absolutely necessary but I think that time has come! *(All exit)*

SCENE CHANGE MUSIC **CD2 Track 17**

SCENE 7: Toad Hall Exterior
(Sarge Stoat and SAS enter.)

Sarge Right, you lot, you're my best men. I'm leaving you in charge of this gate! Only invited persons are to come in tonight! Let's just do a roll call then I'll leave you to it!

Stoats *(Individually)* Brian; Fred; Sam; Jo; Bill; Jon; Kevin.

Tog Special Armed Stoats, the magnificent seven.

Stoats *(Individually)* Strong; Brave; Smooth; Tough; Hand; Some; Charming

Tog Could have been a boy band if we weren't so alarming!

Sarge That's my lads! At ease!

(Mole enters dressed as washerwoman.)

Mole Ooo. You must be <u>so</u> brave.

Sarge Madame, you are not wrong. These boys are the elite SAS – Special Armed Stoats.

Mole Even so, I wouldn't like to be in your shoes tonight, even if they are size 12!

Sarge Why's that then?

Mole My daughter, who washes for Mr Badger, tells me that hundreds of badgers and death or glory toads and rats are coming to sort you out – make sure you leave Toad Hall! I really admire your courage standing in their way! *(Exit)*

Sarge Yeah, well, that's what we do isn't it lads?... Lads!

Stoat 1 *(On mobile phone)* OK Mum, I'll be right there. Sorry Sir, got to go... me Mum wants me back for me tea! *(Exit)*

Stoat 2 I really need the loo. Back later. Maybe tomorrow! *(Exit)*

Stoat 3 I've got a terrible headache come on... *(Exit)*

Stoat 4 I'm with him... *(All remaining Stoats exit)*

Sarge *(In pursuit of exiting Stoats)* Come back! Come back!

SCENE 8: Country Road
(Enter Badger, Ratty, Mole and Toad, dressed for battle.)

Badger So, is everybody sure of the plan? We take the secret tunnel into Toad Hall, which comes up just near where the Chief Weasel is having the worst kept 'surprise' birthday party ever! We'll burst in on them and it'll be more of a shock than a surprise! Mole, clever, clever Mole...

Toad *(Sulkily)* Huh? Seems to me there's nothing very clever about stealing my washerwoman outfit and going and warning the enemy of our plan. Can't see how that's clever at all!

Badger Clever Mole has already put the wind up the guards, so we shouldn't have much trouble from them. So, are we ready? To battle! *(All exit)*

SCENE CHANGE MUSIC **CD2 Track 17**

SCENE 9: Toad Hall Interior

SFX Party **CD2 Track 24**
(Banner goes up again. Enter party group, carrying glasses, wearing party hats. Cries of 'Speech, speech!')

CW Oh I am so very touched. What a lovely surprise this is! I'd like to thank you all for coming...

W1 *(Aside)* Like we had any choice!

CW ...and for all the wonderful gifts which I haven't opened yet, but which I know will be just what I want!

W2 *(Aside)* He should know, he made the list!

CW I'd like to thank my mother and father for having me and I'd particularly like to thank Mr Toad *(Cheer)* for giving us low life the opportunity to enjoy the high life! *(Laughter)*

Song 12 LIFE OF LUXURY *(see Music Book, p79 for lyrics)* **CD Track 14**

(During instrumental verse:)
Weasel 'Ello darling, do you come 'ere often?

Female Oh no – only when the owner's banged up in jail!

Weasel Nice venue for your party, Chief!

CW You're not wrong there! Not so much Toad Hall as 'free for all'!

CW A toast! To the stupidest toad in the whole, wide...

Badger Now! Let's get 'em!

(Ratty, Mole and Badger rush in, with Toad trailing. Keystone cops type chase ensues, with suitable background music. If you would like to use one of the backing tracks, we would suggest 'The Chase-Chase'. The four friends pursue the Wild Wooders, who run off crying out 'Mercy!' 'Help me, mummy' etc. Badger targets Chief, who runs off after a few thwacks! Toad stands bashing them as they exit.)

Badger Hurrah! Good riddance and don't ever think about coming back!

Toad Home at last! Back where I belong. At Toad Hall – the...

All ...finest house on the Riverbank!

Toad Hear! Hear! I say – did you see those leftovers? We can finish them off and I shall make some speeches and...

All No speeches!

Badger Let's just drink a toast together to the Fearsome Four – the new terror of The Wild Wood!

All The Fearsome Four!

Toad And to three of the best friends any fellow could have! Oh, I am a lucky toad!

(During the following narration Ethel and Jeeves enter, carrying gifts for Sally, the Train Driver and Barge Woman and Neddy. They enter and Toad gives each one the relevant gift – clean shirt for Train Driver; flowers for Sally; Oats for Barge Woman and Neddy.)

Narr A lucky Toad, a happy Toad, and dare I say... a sensible Toad – no longer a danger on the roads! A penitent Toad who went back and paid every debt he owed.

Toad Well, well, we did have an adventure, didn't we chaps?!

Ratty We certainly did, Toad old boy, we certainly did!

Mole I rather wish we could do it all again.

Toad Ah now, I did have a thought about aeroplanes! Anybody fancy a nice flight?

All Oh Toad!

Song 13 FRIENDS TOGETHER (FINALE) *(see Music Book, p80 for lyrics)* **CD Track 15**
(During song, cast gather for curtain call – see Song Performance Tips, page 6, for ideas on how to stage this.)

THE END

COPYRIGHT & LICENSING

The world of copyright and licensing can seem rather daunting. Whilst it is a legal requirement for schools to comply with copyright law, we recognise that teachers are extremely busy. For this reason we try to make the process of compliance as simple as possible. The guidelines below explain the most common copyright and licensing issues.

Helpful information can be found on the following website:

A Guide to Licensing Copyright in Schools
www.licensing-copyright.org

And remember, we are always happy to help. For advice simply contact our customer services team:
UK: 01932 232 250 International: +44 1932 232 250 copyright@outoftheark.com

---

General Guidelines

You are free to use the material in our musicals for all **teaching purposes**. However the **performance** of musicals or songs to an audience and the **reproduction** of scripts, lyrics and music scores are subject to licensing requirements by law. The key points are set out below:

Performance of Musicals

The performance of works involving drama, movement, narratives, or spoken dialogue requires a specific licence from the publisher. **** Your PRS licence does not cover musicals ****

We issue affordable licences to schools, churches and nurseries and to simplify the process we include a licence application form with all of our musicals and nativity plays. This can be photocopied and posted or faxed to us.

The performance licence will permit the holder to:

- Perform the musical on the dates applied for.
- Reproduce the song lyrics on printed paper, e.g. for programmes; to make transparencies for overhead projection and to display the lyrics on an interactive whiteboard or other type of screen. The following credit should be included with the lyrics: *'Reproduced by kind permission © Out of the Ark Music'*.
- Photocopy the script for learning purposes. Copies must be destroyed after the performance.
- Make no more than two photocopies of the music score, to be used by participating musicians on the performance dates.

Audio and Video Recordings

If you wish to make an audio or video recording of any of our works please contact us directly:

UK: 01932 232 250 International: +44 1932 232 250 copyright@outoftheark.com

---

Other use of the published material
If you are not staging the musical but still intend to use material from the publication then different licences are required:

Reproduction of Song Lyrics or Musical Scores
The following licences from Christian Copyright Licensing Ltd (www.ccli.com) permit photocopying or reproduction of song lyrics and music scores, for example to create song-sheets, overhead transparencies or to use any electronic display medium.

For UK schools: A Collective Worship Copyright Licence and a Music Reproduction Licence.
For churches: A Church Copyright and Music Reproduction Licence.

Please ensure that you log the songs that are used on your copy report. (Organisations that do not hold one of the above licences should contact Out of the Ark Music directly for permission.)

Performance of Songs
If you are not staging a musical but are performing any of our songs for the public on school premises (i.e. for anybody other than staff and pupils) then royalty payments become due. Most schools have an arrangement with the Performing Rights Society (PRS) through their local authority. Organisations that do not have such an arrangement should contact Out of the Ark Music directly.

LICENCE APPLICATION FORM

(WIND IN THE WILLOWS™)

If you perform **Wind in the Willows™** to an audience other than children and staff you will need to photocopy and complete this form and return it by post or fax to Out of the Ark Music in order to apply for a licence.
If anticipated audience sizes are very small or if special circumstances apply please contact Out of the Ark Music

The licence will permit the holder to:

- Perform *Wind in the Willows* on the dates applied for.
- Reproduce the lyrics to the songs on printed paper, such as for programmes, and to make transparencies for overhead projection. The following credit should be included:
  'Reproduced by kind permission © Out of the Ark Music'.
- Photocopy the script for learning purposes. Copies must be destroyed after the performance.
- Make no more than two copies of the music, to be used by participating musicians on the performance dates.

If the performance is to be recorded please contact Out of the Ark Music.

We wish to apply for a licence to perform *Wind in the Willows* by Mark and Helen Johnson

Customer number (if known): ....

Name of school / organisation: ....

Name of organiser / producer: ....

Date(s) of performance(s): ....

Invoice address: ....

....

Post code: .... **Country:** ....

Telephone number: ....

Number of performances (excl. dress rehearsal)	Performances without admission charges	Performances with admission charges
1	☐ **£23.50*** *[€35.00]*	☐ **£30.00*** *[€45.00]*
2	☐ **£30.00*** *[€45.00]*	☐ **£40.00*** *[€60.00]*
3 or more	☐ **£40.00*** *[€60.00]*	☐ **£50.00*** *[€75.00]*

☐ Tick here if you wish to make an audio or video recording of any of the performance(s).

Tick one of the boxes above. * Prices include VAT. Customers outside the EU will NOT be charged VAT.

Tick one of the four payment options below: *(Invoices will be sent with all licences)*

- ☐ Please bill my school at the above address (UK schools only)
- ☐ I enclose a cheque (Pounds Sterling) for £ .... payable to **Out of the Ark Music**
- ☐ I enclose a cheque (Euro) for € .... payable to **Out of the Ark Music**
- ☐ Please charge the following card: (VISA [not Electron], MasterCard, Maestro & American Express accepted)

Card no:

Start date: _ _ / _ _ (MM/YY)	Expiry date: _ _ / _ _ (MM/YY)	3 digit security code: _ _ _ (last 3 digits on signature strip)

Address: **Out of the Ark Music**
Unit F1 & F2
Kingsway Business Park
Oldfield Road
Hampton
Middlesex
TW12 2HD, United Kingdom

Tel: **020 8481 7200**
Fax: **020 8941 5548**
Email: **info@outoftheark.com**

*The licence fees shown on this form are for **2008-2009** and include VAT at **17.5%**
Prices may be subject to revision

Alice The Musical 7-11s
By Mark & Helen Johnson

This timeless classic is wonderfully retold in a creative combination of song and dance, narrative and drama.

Alice The Musical provides opportunities for solos, unison and 2-3 part singing, in a wide variety of musical styles. It also features composition and improvisation activities which allow children to interact with the score and the script. Includes piano music, lyric sheets, casting tips, staging notes, song recordings and backing tracks.

Titles include:

All In A Golden Afternoon
I'm Late!
Down, Down, Down
I Wish I Hadn't Cried So Much
Caucus Race
Pig And Pepper
Wonderland
Mad As A Hatter
Croquet Dance
Lobster Dance
Who Stole The Tarts?
Off With Her Head!

The Peace Child 7-11s
By Mark & Helen Johnson
and Sue Langwade

Lively songs and a moving script make this the perfect all-year-round musical.

The Peace Child has been thoroughly revised with an updated script by Sue Langwade and contains some of Mark and Helen Johnson's finest songs. Travel to the far away land of Mambica where two opposing tribes seem unwilling to put an end to their enmity. Only the gift of a newborn child can bring peace.

Titles comprise:

Come To The River
Haiy-a! U-Tombya!
Rivial Tribal Song
We'll All Be Famous
Sotongi Strut
Don't Mess With The Bears
Building A Bridge
A Light Has Come
My Life, My Love
Peace Child

Out of the Ark Music
Sefton House, 2 Molesey Road, Hersham Green, Surrey KT12 4RQ, UK
Tel: +44(0)1932 232250, **Fax:** +44(0)1932 703010
Email: info@outoftheark.com **www.outoftheark.com**

Out of the Ark Music